Great Start!

Purchased with
Smart Start Funds

Mm

Kelly Doudna

Published by SandCastle™, an imprint of ABDO Publishing Company, 4940 Viking Drive, Edina, Minnesota 55435.

Printed in the United States.

Cover and interior photo credits: DíAMAR, Digital Stock, Eyewire Images, John Foxx Images, PhotoDisc

Library of Congress Cataloging-in-Publication Data

Doudna, Kelly, 1963-
    Mm / Kelly Doudna.
      p. cm. -- (The alphabet)
    Includes index.
    ISBN 1-57765-406-4
    1. Readers (Primary) [1. Alphabet.] I. Title.

PE1119 .D6762 2000
428.1--dc21
[[E]]   00-028880

The SandCastle concept, content, and reading method have been reviewed and approved by a national advisory board including literacy specialists, librarians, elementary school teachers, early childhood education professionals, and parents.

Let Us Know

After reading the book, SandCastle would like you to tell us your stories about reading. What is your favorite page? Was there something hard that you needed help with? Share the ups and downs of learning to read. We want to hear from you! To get posted on the Abdo Publishing Company Web site, send us email at:

sandcastle@abdopub.com

About SandCastle™

Nonfiction books for the beginning reader

- Basic concepts of phonics are incorporated with integrated language methods of reading instruction. Most words are short, and phrases, letter sounds, and word sounds are repeated.

- Readability is determined by the number of words in each sentence, the number of characters in each word, and word lists based on curriculum frameworks.

- Full-color photography reinforces word meanings and concepts.

- "Words I Can Read" list at the end of each book teaches basic elements of grammar, helps the reader recognize the words in the text, and builds vocabulary.

- Reading levels are indicated by the number of flags on the castle.

Look for more SandCastle books in these three reading levels:

Level 1	Level 2	Level 3
(one flag)	(two flags)	(three flags)

Grades Pre-K to K	**Grades K to 1**	**Grades 1 to 2**
5 or fewer words per page	5 to 10 words per page	10 to 15 words per page

Mary makes a fun friend.

Marcy and Mark
wear masks.

Maria likes milk.

Marty makes a mess.

Matt plays a game.

Mick and Mike
make things.

Mimi makes a call.

Milly hugs her mom.

Where does Molly look?

(mirror)

Words I Can Read

Nouns

A noun is a person, place, or thing

call (KAWL) p. 17
friend (FREND) p. 5
game (GAME) p. 13
masks (MASKSS) p. 7
mess (MESS) p. 11
milk (MILK) p. 9
mirror (MIHR-ur) p. 21
mom (MOM) p. 19
things (THINGZ) p. 15

Proper Nouns

A proper noun is the name
of a person, place, or thing

Marcy (MAR-see) p. 7
Maria (muh-REE-uh) p. 9
Mark (MARK) p. 7

Verbs

A verb is an action or being word

23

More **Mm** Words

map

mittens

moose

mouse

24